MANCHESTE

THE CITY AT A GLANCE

CW01024121

New Century House

GS Hay and Gordon Tait designed th
and-glass HQ complex for the Co-
Century House was added in 1963, a year
after the graceful CIS Tower (see p012).
Corporation Street, T 834 1212

The Arndale

Much Victoriana was wiped out by the 1970s
construction of this vast shopping mall — still
viewed by some as architectural vandalism.
Market Street/Exchange Square

Trinity Bridge

The 1995 pedestrian bridge over the Irwell is
classic Santiago Calatrava. The light, sail-like
structure is balanced by an angled 41m pylon.
St Mary's Parsonage/Brown Street

Albert Bridge House

With its reflective windows and Portland stone
cladding, EH Banks' 1959 tax office building is
a reserved example of Mancunian modernism.
1 Bridge Street

Civil Justice Centre

The award-winning CJC features a 60m-high
glass atrium and cantilevered courtrooms.
See p077

Granada TV

Ralph Tubbs masterminded the 1956 HQ for
Granada. Sadly, its iconic sign is no more as
the operation has been lured to MediaCityUK
and the future of the building is in doubt.
Quay Street

Beetham Tower

Ian Simpson changed the city skyline with
this jagged silhouette in 2006. You can see
the Blackpool Tower from its 23rd-floor bar.
See p013

INTRODUCTION
THE CHANGING FACE OF THE URBAN SCENE

Manchester is a city with attitude. Creativity and expression are valued and praised; pretension is dismantled. Its civic pride and us-versus-them detachment is in part down to the city's archive of 'I was there' moments, from the Sex Pistols' 1976 Lesser Free Trade Hall gig to The Haçienda. But Manchester's transformation into a globally relevant city is about more than music. Ask a local when the regeneration began and many will give an exact date – 15 June 1996. It wasn't any old explosion, that day's IRA bomb: it was the Big Bang. The city is still pushing the boundaries more than 15 years later, with notable triumphs already achieved, such as the Imperial War Museum (see p010) and The Lowry (see p069), sweeping redevelopment in the east and The Quays, and central statements of intent like Piccadilly Basin and the Beetham Tower (see p013).

With its tectonic plates shifting, there's a vitality about the place, and even if locals bemoan and celebrate the changes by turns, big players have taken note – the BBC has moved five departments to MediaCityUK. Manchester's kitchens are urgently striving to win Michelin stars for its epaulette; the service industries have been finally jolted into action; and both the city's football teams are now excelling at the same time. With entrepreneurs finding the gaps in the city's changing urban fabric, creating venues from its stockpile of 19th- and 20th-century buildings, there are no set itineraries. Manchester demands that you come and create your own.

ESSENTIAL INFO
FACTS, FIGURES AND USEFUL ADDRESSES

TOURIST OFFICE
Piccadilly Plaza
Portland Street
T 0871 222 8223
www.visitmanchester.com

TRANSPORT
Car hire
Avis
28 Store Street
T 0844 544 6080
Hertz
Piccadilly Station
T 241 3302
Trams
www.metrolink.co.uk
Trams run Monday to Friday from 7.15am
to 7.30pm; Saturdays from 9.30am to
6pm; and Sundays from 10am to 5pm
Taxis
ManTax
T 230 3333
Radio Cars
T 236 8033
Black cabs can be hailed on the street

EMERGENCY SERVICES
Emergencies
T 999
Police (non-emergencies)
T 872 5050
Late-night pharmacy (until midnight)
Cameo Lord
16 Oxford Street
T 236 1445

EMBASSY
US Embassy
24 Grosvenor Square
London
T 020 7499 9000
london.usembassy.gov

POSTAL SERVICES
Post office
26 Spring Gardens
T 0845 722 3344
Shipping
DHL
85 Halle Mall, The Arndale
T 834 6566

BOOKS
Little Wilson and Big God
by Anthony Burgess (Vintage Classics)
Manchester, England
by Dave Haslam (Fourth Estate)
Rebuilding Manchester
by Euan Kellie (DB Publishing)

WEBSITES
Architecture
www.manchestermodernistsociety.org
Art/Design
www.creativetourist.com
Newspaper
www.menmedia.co.uk

EVENTS
Architecture and Design Festival
www.madf.co.uk
International Festival
www.mif.co.uk

COST OF LIVING
Taxi from airport to city centre
£25
Cappuccino
£2
Packet of cigarettes
£7.10
Daily newspaper
£0.50
Bottle of champagne
£47.50

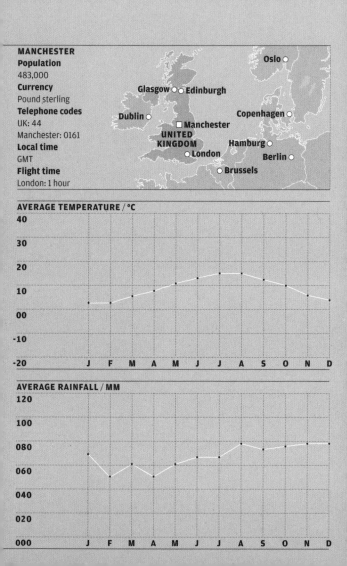

MANCHESTER

Population
483,000

Currency
Pound sterling

Telephone codes
UK: 44
Manchester: 0161

Local time
GMT

Flight time
London: 1 hour

Oslo

Glasgow ○○ Edinburgh

Dublin ○

Copenhagen ○

□ Manchester
UNITED
KINGDOM

Hamburg ○

○ London

Berlin ○

● Brussels

AVERAGE TEMPERATURE / °C

	J	F	M	A	M	J	J	A	S	O	N	D
40
30
20
10
00
-10
-20

AVERAGE RAINFALL / MM

	J	F	M	A	M	J	J	A	S	O	N	D
120
100
080
060
040
020
000

NEIGHBOURHOODS

THE AREAS YOU NEED TO KNOW AND WHY

To help you navigate the city, we've chosen the most interesting districts (see below and the map inside the back cover) and colour-coded our featured venues, according to their location; those venues that are outside these areas are not coloured.

OXFORD ROAD

Home to a wide array of institutions, such as the two universities and the Aquatics Centre (see p094), this corridor connects the centre to Rusholme, Fallowfield and hip Chorlton. Cafés, bars and music venues like The Deaf Institute (see p046) have seen a Southern Quarter label emerge.

PICCADILLY

Thanks to Tadao Ando's pavilion and a fountain plaza by Arup, Piccadilly Gardens is now a serious public space. When all the units at Piccadilly Basin are sold, it should become a vibrant area. For now, flagships are the Ducie Street HQ of architects BDP (responsible for refurbishing the station) and Carver's Warehouse (see p052).

THE QUAYS

The swathe of regenerated dockland lining the Ship Canal would engulf structures of lesser architectural power than The Lowry (see p069) and Imperial War Museum (see p010). The Quays is skewing the city's centre of gravity west, attracting tourists, as well as the BBC to its MediaCityUK.

GAY VILLAGE

Manchester has one of the UK's biggest Gay Pride festivals, with the celebrations ending in the Village. Canal Street, a pathway once favoured for low-profile meetings, has always been its epicentre. The area went mainstream after the 1999 screening of the TV show *Queer as Folk*.

CASTLEFIELD

Located beside the Irwell and pierced by the Rochdale and Bridgewater canals, Castlefield saw some of the city's quickest industrial expansion. It was regenerated in the 1990s but action is now needed once again. Mancunium, a Roman fort near Deansgate, gave the city its name.

CITY CENTRE

Central Manchester is a mixed bag, home to the principal shopping streets, the UK's second largest Chinatown, ancient sites such as Chetham's Library (see p040) and the cathedral, and new kid on the block Urbis (see p068). The Co-operative Group and BDP have drawn up plans to redevelop Victoria station and its environs.

SPINNINGFIELDS

This office and residential development had the misfortune to come into being during the financial crisis, but its retail strip, The Avenue, is now filling up. It's lorded over by the Civil Justice Centre (see p077), while 3 and 4 Hardman Square were designed by Stockport lad Lord Foster.

NORTHERN QUARTER

The building of The Arndale in 1976 was a blow to the Northern Quarter, cutting it off from the city centre. Afflecks – a mini-mall of edgy stores – sums the area up, but it's the proliferation of independent bars, cafés and shops here that makes it the best place in town to do a lot of nothing.

LANDMARKS

THE SHAPE OF THE CITY SKYLINE

It's a kind of architectural beatification when locals nickname a building. The Civil Justice Centre (see p077) quickly became the Filing Cabinet, Hollings Faculty (see p078) is the Toast Rack and the 2005 House of Fraser on Deansgate will always be Kendals. But when developers do similar – Will Alsop didn't call his New Islington building Chips (see p066), Urban Splash did – it grates. Yet to receive a moniker, but hugely symbolic, are Hulme Arch (see p014), which not only has a functional purpose but is a beacon of regeneration, and the monolithic Beetham Tower (see p013). Many still rail against its scale, but residents have started to speak fondly of seeing it from a distance – it means they're nearly home.

The legendary Haçienda was demolished in 2002 and quickly rebuilt as flats, but it was a bungled attempt to represent the former yacht warehouse's curved facade. Fortunately, that other musical pilgrimage site, Salford Lads Club (St Ignatius Walk), which starred on the album sleeve of The Smiths' *The Queen is Dead*, has emerged unscathed. Then there are sprawling buildings that are landmarks because you simply can't avoid them, such as The Arndale (although it's more attractive than it used to be), and Ralph Tubbs' Granada TV complex, which was instantly recognisable for its red lettering: Manchester's take on the Hollywood sign. Now that the logo is gone, it will be interesting to see if the building itself fades from view. *For full addresses, see Resources.*

Imperial War Museum North (IWMN)

Even though his budget was cut by £11m, Daniel Libeskind delivered the goods for the IWMN in 2002. The glistening hulk comprises three symbolic, disjointed steel-and-concrete sections clad in aluminium with a rendered facade. The 55m Air Shard has a viewing platform that affords a vista across the Ship Canal over the city to the Pennines beyond. The Water Shard houses a 160-seat café, and the curved gallery floor of the Earth Shard represents the globe; huge, angled walls are used as a backdrop for hourly sound and light shows. The museum experience may be intended to represent a splintered world, but the architecture sends out a clear, puffed-out-chest message – come to The Quays. *Trafford Wharf Road, T 836 4000, north.iwm.org.uk*

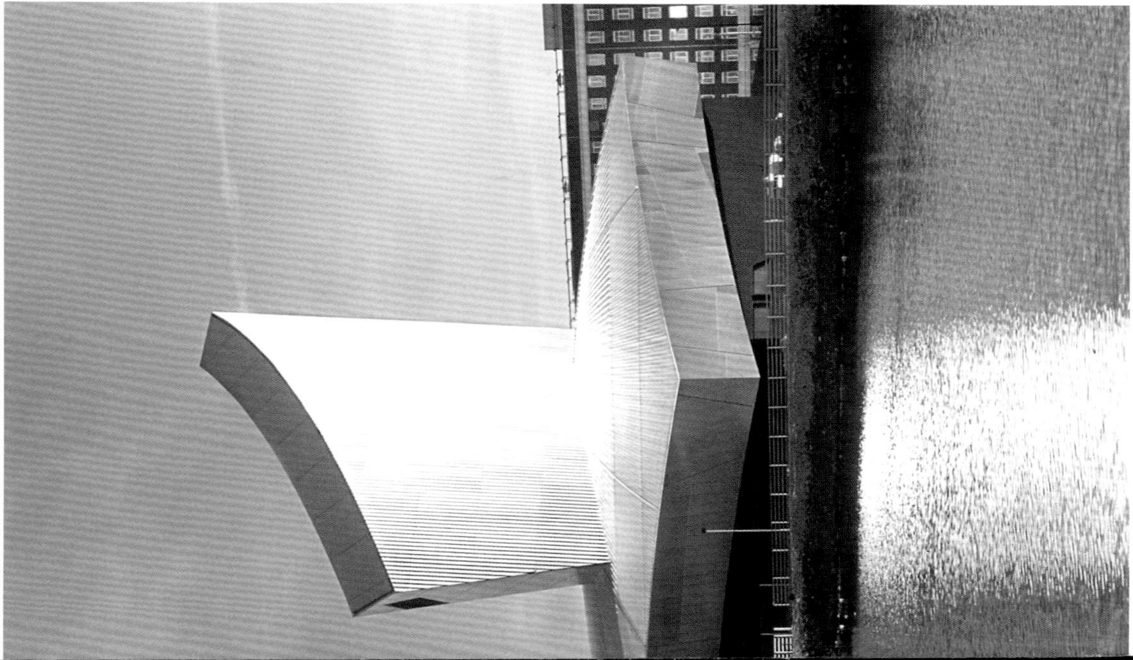

CIS Tower

Designed by GS Hay and Gordon Tait, the 1962 CIS Tower was inspired by SOM's Inland Steel Building in Chicago. At 118m, it was the UK's tallest building outside London for 43 years until the 2006 appearance of the Holloway Circus Tower in Birmingham, which was soon trumped by the Beetham Tower (opposite). The service block was covered in 1 sq cm grey tesserae which started to become unstuck just six months after opening. In 2005, a replacement covering of 7,000 blue solar panels was activated by Tony Blair. The ecological benefits of the refit have been emphasised, but many critics believe that the contrast between the mosaic and the glass curtain walls, aluminium and black enamelled steel of the main office tower was central to the building's appeal.
Miller Street

Beetham Tower

The 169m glass-curtained Beetham Tower became Manchester's tallest structure in 2006. The upper floors are residential and the building's architect Ian Simpson lives in the top-floor penthouse, portraying a cartoonish king-of-all-he-surveys image to those who feel his firm holds too much sway in this city. A Hilton hotel occupies the 23 lower storeys and superlative views can be had from its bar, Cloud 23 (T 870 1600; opens at 5pm), while an adjoining five-storey 'podium' contains event rooms and a restaurant. The switch in the tower's use is signalled by a 4m cantilever which, combined with its slim 10/1 ratio, gives the skyscraper a precarious feel that tempers its lone-wolf cockiness. It may have its tail between its legs if Woods Bagot's delayed 188m Piccadilly Tower goes ahead.
301-303 Deansgate

Hulme Arch

Rolls-Royce set up its first factory in Hulme in the early 20th century but soon moved the operation to Derby. Not much has gone Hulme's way since, including the construction of the Princess Road in 1969 that split the suburb in two, and a housing development inspired by the Royal Crescent in Bath that was a social disaster. Wilkinson Eyre's 1997 bridge reconnected the district across the dual carriageway, both physically and symbolically. Inspired by Eero Saarinen's Missouri Gateway Arch and costing just £2m, it proved a success for the architects, who went on to design a series of BBC buildings at MediaCityUK. With a 52m span, the 25m-high angled arch seems to writhe as you pass. Hulme's regeneration is continuing with MMU's £110m Birley Fields campus, masterminded by Sheppard Robson and slated for 2014.

HOTELS

WHERE TO STAY AND WHICH ROOMS TO BOOK

Manchester's regeneration sketched out the blueprint for a more globally engaged presence, and it was hoped that the major hotel chains would bring their skills to the table. The city is still waiting. Grand plans for the UK's second W hotel and an InterContinental in a Willis Tower-inspired skyscraper were well and truly scuppered by the credit crunch. Although the sleek Hilton Deansgate (303 Deansgate, T 870 1600) did open in the Beetham Tower (see p013), The Lowry (opposite) remains the only real show-stopper.

Of the grandes dames, The Midland (see p026) has the most authenticity; the others fuse contemporary design with features inherited from former industrial incarnations. The Malmaison (Piccadilly, T 278 1000), set in an old linen warehouse, was the city's rock'n'roll hotel when it opened in 1997 – Blakes-lite, in reality – and though the nudge-nudge-wink-wink is a little tired, it's still a solid choice. ABode (see p022) is another warehouse conversion, carried out in some style by designer Mark Plumtree. The new-build Mint (1 Auburn Street, T 242 1000) provides Macs in rooms and a Michael Campbell restaurant. Those looking for a more Mancunian experience should try one of the Eclectic Hotel Collection boutiques in converted Victorian stock – Didsbury House (see p020) and Eleven Didsbury Park (Didsbury Village, T 448 8282) in the 'burbs, and the city-centre Great John Street (see p024). *For full addresses and room rates, see Resources.*

The Lowry Hotel

Named after Salford artist LS Lowry, this 2001 addition to the Rocco Forte portfolio was Manchester's first five-star hotel. The location retains a gritty industrial feel, especially as seen from the Deluxe City View rooms (overleaf), and you may prefer a Riverside Suite for a more pleasant aspect. However, the building's curved glass exterior could not be further from a Lowry painting.

Interiors conceived by Olga Polizzi are complemented by modern artworks – in the lobby (above) are three stone heads by Emily Young and abstract canvases by Ben Cook. Rooms feature an 'Olga' chaise longue and marble bathrooms with Italian porcelain tiling. The restaurant and spa are popular, and the service is exemplary. *50 Dearmans Place, T 827 4000, www.thelowryhotel.com*

Didsbury House

This boutique in the 'burbs has 23 rooms and four suites, each with an individual feel, as much down to the building's burrow-like interior as the design. The hotel was fashioned out of an 1838 Victorian villa and coach house, and has a carved central staircase with an original stained-glass window backlit by a modern atrium (opposite). A Philippe Starck 'Super Archimoon' floor lamp takes pride of place in the lounge. Rooms feature a mix of antique and modern pieces; four have mezzanine levels and 15 have stand-alone roll-top baths (Room 40; above). The best key is for the spacious Opus Loft, which boasts original beams and a fireplace, and two roll-tops side by side. Breakfast is served until everyone's eaten – it's small details like this that make the trip out of town so rewarding.

Didsbury Park, Didsbury Village,
T 448 2200, www.didsburyhouse.co.uk

ABode
This hotel was converted from a Charles
Heathcote warehouse, and a walnutwood
and tiled staircase with art nouveau
light fittings sets the tone for the decor.
The Fabulous on Fifth rooms, such as
Angel Suite 505 (pictured), showcase
the original iron columns and parquet
flooring in loft-style suites, and feature
works by David Hockney and Yoko Ono.
107 Piccadilly, T 247 7744

Great John Street

The Eclectic Hotel Collection runs three boutique properties in the city (see p020), of which Great John Street is its flagship. The hotel makes a feature of its former life as a school, with boys' and girls' staircases, and a headmaster's office turned function space. The gold-and-velvet baroque of the Oyster Bar is no common room, however, and is the setting for one of Manchester's finest afternoon teas. The 30 rooms and suites all have mezzanine levels – the best are the two 58 sq m Opus Grand suites, with antique chandeliers and egg-shaped baths, and the four Eclectic Grand suites (18; left), which feature hand-carved beds and wooden floors. The roof terrace used to be a playground and, with its sun loungers and hot tub, the ethos remains. Sadly, the iconic Granada TV sign that overlooked it was removed in 2010.
Great John Street, T 831 3211,
www.greatjohnstreet.co.uk

The Midland

This hotel was opened by the Midland Railway in 1903, designed by architect Charles Trubshaw; Charles Rolls and Henry Royce first met here the following year, subsequently founding their factory in Hulme (see p014). The hotel underwent a refurbishment for 2006, but many period features remain, such as the cornicework and the wood panelling in the function rooms. The seven Midland Suites are the standouts, notably the four corner ones, which boast high ceilings, a living room and fine views. Standard doubles (above) have a print of a local architectural feature on the headboard. Hotel facilities include a health club and pool, a squash court and The French restaurant, offering consommé and chateaubriand under chandeliers.
Peter Street, T 236 3333,
www.qhotels.co.uk

Radisson Edwardian

The palazzo facade of the old Free Trade Hall (famed for the 'Judas' incident at a Bob Dylan gig in 1966) remains, but when Radisson Edwardian took over the site in 2004, the body of Leonard C Howitt's building (see p078) was controversially demolished and rebuilt. Rooms and suites are named after those who performed here – Dylan, of course, Ella Fitzgerald, Shirley Bassey and the US entertainer

Danny Kaye (above; an Al Fresco suite with a decked veranda). Manchester-born Michael Attenborough became RE's head of design in 1999 and introduced black lacquered paintwork, oriental artefacts and natural materials. The hotel's Sienna spa and Opus One restaurant are some of the sleekest spots in the city. *Peter Street, T 835 9929, www.radissonedwardian.com/manchester*

The Light

To the extent that this is a city with attitude (Mancunians don't do fawning), apartment hotels are an appropriate choice. The quality is rather hit and miss, however, and too often staff are not so much behind the scenes, but actually AWOL. One of the most reliable properties is The Light, on the cusp of the Northern Quarter, with on-hand staff, a gym and spa facilities; penthouses (above) have a hot tub. On the downside, the interior of the Conran & Partners design has become shabby in places. Other options include the Maxima and Penthouse suites offered by Roomzzz on Princess Street (T 236 2121), with original wooden floors, iron girders and skylights, and Staying Cool's Fresh and Woody apartments (T 0121 285 1250).
20 Church Street, T 839 4848,
www.thelight.co.uk

Velvet

The 1999 TV series *Queer as Folk* changed the dynamic of Canal Street – hen parties and women arrived first, quickly followed by straight men. Velvet originally opened as a bar and restaurant with a European menu to cater for this new social mix, and added 19 rooms in 2009. Designers RCA maintained the character of the former mill, with sandblasted brick, heavy timber beams and cast-iron columns. The quasi-industrial feel is set off by the furnishings, such as Osborne & Little wallpaper and the eponymous velvet (fortunately used sparingly). Each room offers a different experience – Velvet King 12 (left) features a large photo of a Mexican artwork. We'd opt for a room on the third floor, some of which have balconies, as the elevation means you are spared the full blast of one of the city's hardest-partying streets.
2 Canal Street, T 236 9003,
www.velvetmanchester.com

24 HOURS

SEE THE BEST OF THE CITY IN JUST ONE DAY

It's fitting that we should start our 24 hours of history-dipping (it's unavoidable in this city) in *24 Hour Party People* territory – the Northern Quarter, home of Factory Records and its legendary Dry bar (28 Oldham Street, T 236 9840). However, the area's edginess has mostly gone, so have a cuppa instead at North Tea Power (opposite). From 'Madchester', change tack to another of the city's sobriquets, Cottonopolis. These days, the Town Hall (see p034) is as well turned out as the Victorian ladies who once graced its stairs, but the cotton trade's role in its no-expense-spared construction is far from spotless. Many other Victorian buildings have been converted into modern venues. An old fish market houses the Craft & Design Centre (see p036); the basement of Charles Heathcote's warehouse is home to one of the city's best restaurants (see p037); there's the children's shelter that's become a watering hole (see p044); and a chapel turned quirky music hall (see p046).

In stark contrast to all the red brick, take time out to visit the ancient Chetham's Library (see p040) and, nestled among the city's heavy industry, bold contemporary builds such as a ski slope (see p042) and arts centre The Lowry (see p069). The decadent, round-the-clock party scene is harder to find these days, especially on week nights; Berlin-style dive The Corner (254 Wilmslow Road, T 224 8356) and Corridor (see p054) are our tips for last port of call. *For full addresses, see Resources.*

10.00 North Tea Power

Hip tea rooms abound in the Northern Quarter, which is home to Teacup and Cakes (see p062), Bread and Butter (T 07944 607 405) and North Tea Power, which is bringing back a little of the leaf's exoticism. Try the Darjeeling latte, perhaps accompanying a breakfast of Norlander bread with wildflower honey followed by a delicious slice of florentine. Of his many interesting brews, co-owner Wayne Lew also recommends the cascara coffee cherry infusion. The venue is adorned with reclaimed materials, such as a table fashioned from scaffolding boards and shelving from trees felled due to Dutch elm disease. Rotating exhibitions are of a consistently high standard. Note that the café opens at 11am on Sundays. *36 Tib Street, T 833 3073, www.northteapower.co.uk*

11.00 Town Hall

Liverpudlian architect Alfred Waterhouse needed all his nous to squeeze this 1877 neo-Gothic marvel into a cramped triangular site. The soot that long blackened the building was symbolic of Manchester's industry, but Waterhouse's design speaks of it too – it was cotton that made the city wealthy, and the mosaic floor is embellished with stylised flowers and bees, while roundels depict a weaver and spinner. The impressive interior features three stone spiral staircases and a groin-vaulted Great Hall with murals by pre-Raphaelite painter Ford Madox Brown. Emanuel Vincent Harris designed the 1938 neo-Gothic extension. One wall curves in sympathy with the circular Central Library, and two covered bridges connect it to the Town Hall. Tours can be booked in advance.
Albert Square, T 234 3555

12.00 Craft & Design Centre

The noise and commotion of this glass-roofed Victorian fish market was replaced by a low hum of artisanship and appreciation when it became the Craft & Design Centre in 1982. It contains around 20 studio-shops, including those of Jane Blease, whose lightboxes and embroidered wood veneer lampshades have won awards; Linzi Ramsden's unique organic and geometric ceramics; and textile artist Moira Walton's handmade books inspired by found objects and ephemera. The food at the C&D Centre café is homemade, naturally. On a similar tip, the Manchester Craft Mafia (an offshoot of the Austin, Texas, company) is a collective of local makers that distributes online and within Greater Manchester. *17 Oak Street, T 832 4274, www.craftanddesign.com*

13.00 Michael Caines Restaurant

The ABode Hotels venture is a successful partnership between chef Michael Caines and Andrew Brownsword, who gives his initials to the rapidly expanding UK chain. At Caines' restaurant in the Manchester hotel (see p022), executive chef Mark Rossi and sommelier Michael Sokolov consistently excel. The former nightclub was refitted by Mark Plumtree of Yorkshire design firm MPDA, and features walnut joinery, a slate bar and private booths behind voile curtains. At weekends, Caines cooks at his two-Michelin-starred Gidleigh Park restaurant in Devon, while during the week he puts in shifts at the various ABode offshoots. The seven-course tasting menu is recommended, as is the fabulous-value lunch.
ABode Hotel, 107 Piccadilly, T 200 5678, www.michaelcaines.com

14.30 Richard Goodall Gallery

The music-oriented RG Gallery launched in Thomas Street (T 832 3435) in 2000 with '33 Still Lives' by photographer Anton Corbijn. It has since broadened its remit to include contemporary painting, silkscreen gig and film posters by artists such as Jay Ryan, and limited-edition urban vinyl figures by the likes of Frank Kozik. Its success led to the opening of this second space, in a white cube around the corner, in 2007. It has exhibited work by Leonard Cohen, Ray Caesar, Mat Daly and John Lennon, with other shows curated by theme, such as 'FAC 51 The Haçienda', which featured memorabilia related to the legendary nightclub. Gered Mankowitz's lenticular prints sell well for the gallery. *103 High Street, T 834 3330, www.richardgoodallgallery.com*

15.30 Chetham's Library

Established in 1653 according to the will of textile merchant Humphrey Chetham, this library was intended to rival those at Oxbridge. Housed in a 1421 building, Chetham's is the oldest free public library in the world, and many historical figures have studied here ('The stained-glass window ensures that the weather is always fine,' wrote Engels) on carved oak stools below an arched, timbered ceiling (above).

The mark on the Audit Room table is said to have been made when occultist Dr John Dee accidentally summoned the devil, who appeared hoof first. The library is open weekdays 9am-4.30pm (closed for lunch). Tours, which include the cloisters and the Baronial Hall, are arranged through the Music School (T 834 9644) next door.
Long Millgate, T 834 7961,
www.chethams.org.uk

16.30 Chill Factore

The flat landscape beside the M60 bears some remarkable interventions: the white confection of the Trafford Centre, the engineering marvel of Davyhulme wastewater treatment plant and, since 2007, Chill Factore, which is a 15-minute taxi ride from the city centre. The FaulknerBrowns development offers the longest indoor ski slope in the UK and although, at 180m, it may be completed in a matter of seconds by accomplished riders, the range of activities on offer is impressive. There's race training, freestyle and airbag sessions with pro skiers and boarders, sledging and even a luge run. Perfect for a shot of adrenaline before a night out. Book online to take advantage of the fast-track service.

Trafford Quays Leisure Village, Trafford Way, T 749 2222, www.chillfactore.com

19.00 The Gaslamp

Originally the kitchen of an 1860s children's street mission — see the sculpted heads of cheery kids high up on the terracotta exterior — The Gaslamp has a fine heritage of sating needy souls. The two glazed-brick rooms feel a little like a Victorian mortuary, but the edges are softened by natural wood, photos detailing the site's history and works by local artists hung throughout. The focus is on liquid nourishment, with rotating guest ales, including some fine pints from the Kirkstall brewery in Leeds. Regular live jazz and blues gigs and the cured meat platters are further draws. Beer aficionados should also try The King's Arms (T 832 3605) or The Mark Addy (see p048), both just over the Irwell. *50a Bridge Street, T 478 1224, www.thegaslamp.co.uk*

20.30 The Alchemist

In 2010, local firm Living Ventures opened The Alchemist in an L-shaped block that sits flush with Spinningfields' offices and chain eateries. The interior by legendary Salford designer Trevor Johnson (Factory Records, The Haçienda) features an antique apothecary cabinet, dark polished wood, an oak bar and hanging lights that evoke hi-tech creepers. The flavours coming out of the kitchen are big and satisfying, with dishes such as blackened sea bass fillet and jerk chicken with dumplings. The 'molecular' cocktails include a lavender and coconut daiquiri and shooters served in test-tube glasses. If you can't get a table here, Kiwi chef Paul Greening conjures up fine Pacific Rim-style dining at nearby Australasia (T 831 0288). *3 Hardman Street, T 817 2950, www.thealchemist.uk.com*

22.30 The Deaf Institute
The nights at this bar and music venue
are anything but regular. Take Thursdays'
Reykjavik Tourist Guide, for example, a DJ
set with music inspired by the Icelandic
landscape. The Deaf Institute, along with
Sandbar (T 273 1552), Odder (T 238 9132)
and The Cornerhouse (see p064), have
contributed to the coining of a 'Southern
Quarter' label. Designed by Forster Inc,
the ground floor and basement house
a café and cocktail bar respectively, with
wallpaper by Saint Honoré and Timorous
Beasties, and an arresting speaker stack
(right). The first-floor music hall features
a domed skylight and tiered seating that
survive from John Lowe's 1877 building,
and the space is thought to have served
as a chapel. Above the main entrance is
an engraving of a hand over a book – the
emblem on badges worn by the deaf.
135 Grosvenor Street, T 276 9350,
www.thedeafinstitute.co.uk

URBAN LIFE

CAFÉS, RESTAURANTS, BARS AND NIGHTCLUBS

There's a ready-made VIP clientele of football and soap opera stars for the city's high-end dining venues, many of which are found in the top hotels. But it's worth using a little imagination, as although Manchester's lack of a Michelin star provokes much soul-searching among local gastronomes, there's a laudable trend towards modern British cuisine, with Vertigo (opposite) leading the way. Two of the best-looking restaurants, Rosso (43 Spring Gardens, T 832 1400), within the blue-streaked marble of a former bank, and Stock (4 Norfolk Street, T 839 6644), in the old exchange, can be let down by inconsistency. Also opening in a former financial institution, in late 2011, Jamie's Italian in the Midland Bank (see p064) might shake things up. Conversely, Robert Owen Brown's cooking makes up for the now-tired canalside location at The Mark Addy (Stanley Street, T 832 4080). Or head to the suburbs to the excellent Lime Tree (8 Lapwing Lane, T 0871 811 4873) in West Didsbury.

The puffed-up republic-of-Mancunia mentality of the 1990s is no more. However, shabby chic still rules at musically minded venues such as Corridor (see p054), Cord (see p059) and jazz-led Matt and Phred's (64 Tib Street, T 831 7002). The long-running club Sankeys (Beehive Mill, Radium Street, T 236 5444) now puts on trance, techno, house and dubstep. For a more rounded edge, there's the opulence of Cinnabar (see p058) and Obsidian (see p060).
For full addresses, see Resources.

Vertigo

Adopting the maxim 'if it ain't broke', Vertigo moved into this space in 2011 and barely touched its five floors of bling (all black and sultry, with cascading chandeliers and velvet furnishings) created by previous occupants Ithaca, the celeb-courting Japanese restaurant. The menu, however, received a volte-face, and chef Ian Armstrong presents outstanding UK cuisine that is robust, straight-talking and seasonal. The Yorkshire Middle White pork with Bury black pudding, apple foam and quince jus showcases a commitment to traceability; the 'rabbit in an English garden' starter combines superior flavours and playful presentation; and the grilled lobster confirms a kitchen that can exploit the richness of regional ingredients.
*36 John Dalton Street, T 839 9907,
www.vertigomanchester.co.uk*

NoHo
This former clothing warehouse, with
its huge windows, parquet flooring
and retro seating, is decorated with
apocalyptic graffiti by the Upper Space/
Sketch City collective. The hip bolthole
opens at 5pm. Retro board games lie
around, films are projected onto the
back wall and DJs play at weekends.
Spear Street, Stevenson Square,
T 236 5381, www.noho-bar.com

An Outlet

On the ground floor of Carver's Warehouse, a conversion of Manchester's oldest stone building (dated 1806) and one of Piccadilly Basin's flagship developments, An Outlet is decked out simply with natural wood finishes, blackboard menus and fairy lights. Owners Four23 describe it as a 'traditional coffeehouse – a space to congregate, plot, write and entertain', inspired by the legendary Greenwich Village venue Caffe Cino. Books such as Yoko Ono's *Grapefruit* and *Scandinavian Modern Furnishings 1930-1973* are left lying around; there are monthly lunchtime lectures from Manchester Business School over, say, a beetroot, bacon and Lancashire cheese salad; and evening entertainment includes film nights, and gigs by the likes of Wu Lyf. *77 Dale Street, T 236 3043, www.anoutlet.net*

Aumbry

With just a handsome old dresser and a few roses for ornamentation, the living room of this converted cottage underlines what a bare transaction dining out is: you pay people to cook for you. In this case, it's married chefs Laurence Tottingham and Mary-Ellen McTague, whose training under Heston Blumenthal results in inspired plating and, invariably, excellence. The fact that there are only 26 covers and a succinct menu makes each item from the tiny kitchen seem all the more special. Readiness of local produce informs the dishes, which incorporate forage foods when available. We suggest the Inglewhite pork from Tom Parkinson's Lancashire farm, Aumbry's own air-dried hams and Bury black pudding Scotch eggs.
2 Church Lane, Prestwich, T 798 5841, www.aumbryrestaurant.co.uk

Corridor

This cocktail bar has an impeccable reputation, yet manages to retain its speakeasy vibe. It helps that it's tricky to find – Barlows Croft is barely wider than a corridor – and the basement of exposed brick, green glass shelves and a deep-red glow feels appropriately illicit and liminal. The licensing regulations are looser here too, enabling Corridor to stay open until 4am. Owner Ian Morgan's cocktails have won awards – try the Fool's Gold (when in Rome...), which blends tequila, dark chocolate, orange and bitters. On Saturdays, Cosmic Disco's Mark Webster is a regular fixture on the decks. Another Barlows Croft delight is a cut-through at the bottom of the alley to Santiago Calatrava's Trinity footbridge. *6-8 Barlows Croft, Salford, T 832 6699, www.corridorbar.co.uk*

Albert's Shed

When he opened this venue in 2004, Jim Ramsbottom named it in honour of his great uncle Albert, who was a labourer when derelict Castlefield was redeveloped in the early 1990s and this site functioned as a tool shed. Architect Roger Stephenson was sensitive to the area's character when designing the restaurant, using brick in keeping with the warehouses, and pre-weathered zinc to mirror the slate roofs.

The menu is British with a few Italian dishes, served in a clean-lined, airy interior. Eat on the terrace, where the panorama of the canal basin and railway bridge offers a gritty Mancunian alfresco. Albert's Shed is a consistent performer in Castlefield, whose 1990s optimism, epitomised by Mick Hucknall's Barça (T 839 7099), has waned. *20 Castle Street, T 839 9818, www.albertsshed.com*

Isinglass

It's well worth the 10-minute drive out of town to the Victorian suburbs, where twins Anthony Dunbar (chef) and Rachel Ireland (front of house) have run Isinglass since 2010. The name – an archaic term for fish-bladder gelatin – may raise the spectre of culinary alchemy, but the menu is steadfastly down to earth. Dunbar sources local goods such as Cumbrian charcuterie, Lancastrian cheese and plenty of Cheshire produce, and the menu features dishes like razor clams, venison Wellington and sticky toffee pudding with pecan brittle and ice cream from a farm in Tatton. Cushion-strewn banquettes, well-worn floorboards and pub-like tables decorated with herbs make for a laidback, homely experience.

46 Flixton Road, Urmston, T 749 8400, www.isinglassrestaurant.co.uk

Vermilion and Cinnabar

Built at a cost of £5.2m, Manchester's most expensively assembled restaurant has good company in the Newton Heath/Miles Platting 'burbs – one of the world's most expensively assembled football teams, Manchester City, play at nearby Etihad Stadium. The venue's 'retro-futuristic' design is by Miguel Câncio Martins, responsible for the Buddha Bar in Paris. The high-end Thai restaurant Vermilion (above) has fibreglass coral-shaped pillars, copper tables, marble floors and lighting by Firefly, while Cinnabar is decked out with 'cocoon booths' – imagine the 1987 film *Innerspace* and substitute a lava lamp for the human body. The local International 3 gallery has helped transform a second-floor function room into a Vox art space. *Hulme Hall Lane/Lord North Street, T 202 0055, www.vermilioncinnabar.com*

Cord

The 2008 refit of this institution saw its corduroy wall-lining removed. It must have been like ripping off a second skin for Cord's clientele, who can lay claim to being Northern Quarter pioneers. When the bar was founded in 2001 this area had a distinct edge, and Cord, with a music policy informed by such regulars as Badly Drawn Boy and Andy Votel, helped to make it a viable late-night destination. The white tiles in the cellar remain, offset with neo-baroque furniture and Daren Newman illustrations, but while Cord has spruced itself up, it has kept the alehouse mindset and remains a hub of cool – Primal Scream bassist Mani is among those hosting monthly nights here. The owners also run nearby restaurant Thomas (T 839 7033). *8 Dorsey Street, T 832 9494, www.cordbar.com*

Obsidian

Descend the Italian marble staircase below the 1878 Dugdale's warehouse to the flash Obsidian. Following a redesign in 2008, it has a colour palette of lilac, beige and gold, a 15m-long frosted, back-lit glass bar, a granite floor and four 'champagne' booths. The seasonal cocktail list includes the English Country Garden, a Hendrick's gin and cucumber martini with lemon, mint, honey and apple juice that will give you rosy cheeks, and on cold nights try the Grounds for Divorce (named after a song by Bury band Elbow), a rich bourbon infused with figs. The menu focuses on seasonal British produce, such as fillet of beef with ox cheek tortellini and crispy tongue and a salad of heirloom tomatoes with orange, mint and almond crisp.
24 Princess Street, T 238 4348,
www.obsidianmanchester.co.uk

INSIDER'S GUIDE

PETE MASTERS, FURNITURE DESIGNER

Hulme resident Pete Masters is a furniture-maker and an interior designer (www.mrmasters.co.uk), who has worked with Oi Polloi (see p081) and Selfridges. Mr Scruff's café Teacup and Cakes (55 Thomas Street, T 832 3233) serves as Masters' makeshift office and when he has lunch there he'll often order the meatballs and pesto sauce. Another favourite café is Kim By The Sea (49 Old Birley Street, T 232 7667). 'They serve proper home cooking,' he says. 'The vegetables are grown over the road.' A fan of all things retro, Masters suggests Haworth in West Yorkshire for its vintage fairs and stores such as Eyres 'N' Graces (75 Main Street, T 01535 643 444).

In the evening, he might pop in to Port Street Beer House (39-41 Port Street, T 237 9949) or Mr Thomas's Chop House (52 Cross Street, T 832 2245), a restored 1867 pub and restaurant. 'It's like walking into the 19th century.' For a smart dinner, he heads to San Carlo Cicchetti (King Street West, T 839 2233) to sample its 'fabulous pizzas and hams' or Australasia (see p045): 'You enter through a glass triangle.' He DJs on Saturdays at the Cornerhouse (see p064), spinning 1960s rock and R&B, and knows the local scene well. His top tips are The Deaf Institute (see p046) and El Diablo's Social Club (www.eldiablos.co.uk), an occasional underground night held at interesting venues, including Victoria Baths (see p071): 'Really good DJs play, often under a pseudonym.' *For full addresses, see Resources.*

ARCHITOUR
A GUIDE TO MANCHESTER'S ICONIC BUILDINGS

A mass of Victoriana – both functional and flamboyant – lines Manchester's streets, which were described by German author WG Sebald in *The Emigrants* as 'dark ravines'. But the city now has a far brighter future. In the wake of the 1996 IRA bomb, its desire to regenerate kickstarted an era of wholesale modernisation.

The most recent wave has seen the ambition of the New Islington (see p066) and Piccadilly Basin projects, the latter by architects Ian Simpson. Then there are smaller-scale schemes, such as a 2014 home for the Cornerhouse arts centre (70 Oxford Street, T 228 7621) on nearby First Street, designed by Mecanoo, and Austin-Smith Lord's People's History Museum (Left Bank, T 838 9190), with its curved Cor-ten facade. Located beside the Civil Justice Centre (see p077), it's like a beauty spot on the courthouse's perfect skin.

Unusually, much of Manchester's architectural stock has been well preserved or restored rather than demolished. A highlight is Edwin Lutyens' compact yet soaring art deco Midland Bank (100 King Street), dating from 1935. It was refurbished by Stephenson Bell, and the superb hall now serves as a restaurant (see p048). Manchester also boasts great modernist buildings. As well as the 'Toast Rack' (see p078), view the Crown Courts (Crown Square), also designed by Leonard C Howitt, the CIS Tower (see p012) and any number of the faculties on the former UMIST campus.
For full addresses, see Resources.

Universal Church of the Kingdom of God
Edgar Wood, an exponent of the Arts and Crafts movement, never received as much recognition as contemporaries like Charles Rennie Mackintosh. Completed in 1906, Wood's Christian Scientists church is designed in an unusual Y-shape, which funnels visitors towards an entrance that opens beneath a long, steep gable with canted walls folded back like wings, and a stone chimney rising to one side. Inside, there's a play of colour and detail from the *mashrabiya* organ screen to the reredos panel on either side of the space. Closure in the 1970s left the building vandalised before becoming the Edgar Wood Centre (1975-2003), then a UCKG in 2008. Entry is only possible during a service.
71 Daisy Bank Road, Victoria Park

Chips

Will Alsop's brightly coloured mixed-use stack is the flagship of New Islington, a beacon of sustainable regeneration on the former 1970s Cardroom sink estate, 10 minutes' walk from Piccadilly station. Nine storeys high, 100m long and ringed by canals, Chips' timber cladding bears the names of north-western waterways in huge type. Inevitably, it has drawn criticism from the traditionalists, who regard it as throwaway architectural self-indulgence; an accusation compounded by some poor finishing. Other New Islington developments of note are DMFK's Guest Street and the self-design project Tutti Frutti, inspired by West 8's Borneo Sporenburg in Amsterdam, which manages to be even more kitsch than Chips.

2 Lampwick Lane, www.newislington.co.uk

Urbis

Architects Ian Simpson did well to make this building work, as it had to be squeezed between a heavyweight urban medley of The Printworks entertainment complex, the Triangle shopping mall, the cathedral and Chetham's (see p040). Urbis also came to be seen as a kind of architectural retort, located 100m from the site of the 1996 terrorist attack. Clad with 2,200 glass panels, Urbis looks like the Flatiron Building sculpted in ice. It began life in 2002 as an exhibition centre devoted to the 'urban experience' but has now been transformed into the National Football Museum, whose doors open in early 2012, displaying memorabilia such as Maradona's 'Hand of God' shirt and the 1966 World Cup Final ball.
Cathedral Gardens, T 870 9275, www.nationalfootballmuseum.com

The Lowry

Many of LS Lowry's paintings depict looming industrial landscapes, and if any corner of Manchester can make you feel small, it's The Quays, the site of this Michael Wilford-designed theatre complex and exhibition space. A decision was taken in 1988 to found a new arts centre here and when a £64m National Lottery grant was secured in 1996 (20 years after Lowry's death), the city council called it 'Salford's greatest day in living memory'. Firmly rooted to its triangular footprint by 803 concrete pillars, The Lowry has a maritime feel, with porthole windows and gangway-like landings. The glass-and-steel exterior reflects the surroundings; inside, Wilford's characteristic use of bright colours is in evidence. A footbridge over the Ship Canal connects it to the IWMN (see p010).
Pier 8, T 0843 208 6000, www.thelowry.com

City Airport

Development of the Barton Moss site began in 1928, with Imperial Airways commencing UK-based flights in 1930 from what was one of the world's first municipal passenger airports. It was a bunting-strewn visitor attraction of its time, and Cobham's Flying Circus was among the draws in 1932. The original octagonal brick-and-concrete control tower was refurbished in 2006 and this structure, together with the hangar and terminal building (a late 19th-century farm conversion, roofed with Welsh slate) are Grade II listed. Visitors can access the control tower's first floor, and a hut houses an exhibition on the airport's history. It is now used as a private airfield and is home to a number of flying schools.
Liverpool Road, Eccles, T 789 1362, www.cityairportltd.com

Victoria Baths

Designed by Henry Price and opened in 1906, Victoria Baths is an architectural study in the British class system. Water from the baths' artesian well first filled the 23m (then Olympic-size) First Class male pool (above) before recycling into a Second Class males' and ending up in the Female pool. Entrance fees were lowest on the 'dirty day' before the weekly water change. The décor is most striking in the main male entrance, with its fish-pattern mosaic floor and locally fired emerald tiling. Stained-glass windows detail sporting figures. The facilities throughout were of a high quality, and segregation was phased out after a decade. Since its 1993 closure, volunteers have campaigned for its restoration and offer weekly tours.
Hathersage Road, Chorlton-on-Medlock, T 224 2020, www.victoriabaths.org.uk

Daily Express Building

Sir Owen Williams worked with Ellis and Clarke on the Daily Express Building in London, but in Manchester he had more autonomy and space. With wide roads on all sides, the triple-height press rooms received plentiful light, allowing pedestrians to peer in at the workers, encased behind black Vitrolite. The 1939 building lacks the art deco ornament of its Fleet Street counterpart, but its accessibility arguably makes it superior. The paper quit the premises in the late 1980s, when mirror film was added to the windows in order to prepare the building for office use. The interior now features an atrium and apartments on the upper storeys, but the striking rounded corners and beautiful jet-and-silver exterior are unchanged.
19 Great Ancoats Street

John Rylands Library

Enriqueta Rylands' neo-Gothic memorial to her husband opened in 1900. Designed by Basil Champneys, it has been part of the University of Manchester since 1972, and houses rare books and manuscripts. Mrs Rylands splashed out on materials and mod cons – sandstone, Polish oak, bronze fixtures and fittings, sculptures by John Cassidy and a pollution-filtering system. A refurbishment between 2003 and 2008 by Austin-Smith Lord saw a timber-trussed pitched roof built over the Reading Room, which is cloistered away from the noise of the street, and a five-storey, glass-fronted extension (opposite), which now serves as the entrance (above). The library hosts exhibitions curated from the collection as well as guided tours.
150 Deansgate, T 306 0555,
www.library.manchester.ac.uk

Barton Arcade

The tiled floor and original shopfronts are gone and the exterior isn't all that, but the 1871 Barton Arcade is a must-see even in its bare bones. Indebted to the techniques pioneered by Joseph Paxton for the Crystal Palace, Corbett, Raby and Sawyer used iron from W Macfarlane & Co's Saracen Foundry in Glasgow. The two glass domes produce a 16m interior full of light. Establishment cobblers Edwards (T 834 1339) is here, as is members' bar The Circle Club (T 288 8118), but even if you've no interest in shopping it's worth exploring the three balconies for their delicately worked wrought-iron balustrades and mahogany handrails. Be grateful it's still here – other arcades of the period, such as the one in the Victoria Buildings, are no more.
St Ann's Square/Deansgate,
www.bartonarcade.com

Civil Justice Centre

The investment of £113m in a 16-storey building with no commercial function is a powerful symbol of a self-confident city. The 2007 Civil Justice Centre, with its 47 courtrooms and 75 consultation rooms, is the largest such complex to be built in the UK since the 1882 Royal Courts of Justice in London. Australian firm Denton Corker Marshall's design even succeeds in being rather fun (a far cry from the usual courtroom architecture), with its cantilevering glass segments, like drawers pulled out from a desk, and the light flooding the building. Spaces in the central bulk are kept bright thanks to high clerestory windows, and yellow and grey mixed-purpose pods seem to dangle off the sides of the impressive 11-storey atrium.

Gartside Street, T 240 5000

Hollings Faculty

Leonard C Howitt's Hollings College (1957-60) was quickly dubbed the 'Toast Rack' by locals – appropriate then, that its parabolic arches should house the Domestic and Trades College, and are now home to Manchester Met's food, tourism and clothing faculty. It was one of the first buildings in the city to reject any reference to past styles, as Howitt explored the expressive potential of concrete, and the ensemble includes a low, round block (the 'Fried Egg'), housing a restaurant in which students can practise, and a curved hall used for fashion shows. Howitt was also responsible for a well-received reconstruction of the bombed Free Trade Hall in 1951 (see p027). Further fine 1960s examples of educational modernism include the Renold Building by WA Gibbon and HS Fairhurst's Chemical Engineering Pilot Plant, both in Sackville Street.
Old Hall Lane

SHOPPING
THE BEST RETAIL THERAPY AND WHAT TO BUY

The opening of Selfridges and Harvey Nichols in Exchange Square skewed the Manchester shopping scene for a few years as it fell in love with fancy labels. They're still pulling in the crowds, but the sprucing-up of The Arndale, the opening of the Trafford Centre and The Avenue at Spinningfields, and the post-recession recovery of King Street – dubbed the 'Bond Street of the North' – and nearby St Ann's Square and Barton Arcade (see p076), whose independent boutiques fared better, means that the choices have multiplied.

Wayne and Gerardine Hemingway opened one of the first Red or Dead outlets in Afflecks (52 Church Street, T 839 0718), and the Northern Quarter is still where indies cut their teeth, among them womenswear boutique Curiouser & Curiouser (70 Tib Street, T 835 4068) and Renegade Marmalade (see p086), which moved to King Street in 2011. To see work by other Mancunian labels and designers, head to the Saturday Tib Street fashion market.

Traditional men's tailoring is well represented by old-school stores, such as the shirtmaker Frank Rostron (39 Princess Street, T 236 5379). For more bespoke, A Few Fine Things (7 Oak Street, T 832 8400) creates stylish bags using British leather and fasteners from one of the UK's few remaining buckle-making companies, while Dutch & Wolf (Thornfield House, Delamer Road, Bowdon, T 927 2750) sells hand-built bikes from its Cheshire showroom. *For full addresses, see Resources.*

Oi Polloi

Staying true to its Northern Quarter roots, Oi Polloi's current store is minutes away from the Tib Street address where Steve Sanderson and Nigel Lawson set up shop in 2002. The thrust is British sportswear and classic, functional outdoor clothing, including Manchester labels Henri Lloyd and Baracuta. Oi Polloi also had a hand in introducing brands such as Fjällräven and Yuketen to the UK. The shop-fit by Pete Masters (see p062) is Scandinavian inspired, utilising ash, pitch pine cladding and furniture from salvage yards and antiques fairs. The store's own brand, Cottonopolis, launched in 2011 with a range of Italian knitwear and English-manufactured jackets and belts. The key piece is a locally made four-pocket parka. *63 Thomas Street, T 831 7870, www.oipolloi.com*

Levenshulme Antiques Village
The 1898 Levenshulme town hall, with its original tiling and mosaic floors, is crammed full of antiques dealers over three storeys. Look out for Johnson's, specialising in Victorian and Edwardian furniture in mahogany and oak; Rick's Place, for 1950s and 1960s glass, fine porcelain and phonographs; and antiquarian-book dealer Ken Morrison.
965 Stockport Road, T 225 7025

James Darby

Tailor James Darby started out by unpicking and restyling secondhand clothes and wearing them around town. He caught the eye of established Manchester shirtmaker Frank Rostron (see p080), who hired him as an apprentice. In 2003, Darby opened his off-the-peg retail outlet and workshop in the Northern Quarter, and moved to these premises in 2009, decked out with vintage furniture, and using recycled doors for the cutting table and shelving. Look out for his Manchester mac, which is made from Ventile, a fabric created at Didsbury's Shirley Institute in the 1930s to protect RAF pilots shot down over water. Darby has also made scarves for Paul Weller, and describes his mod aesthetic as 'tapered and architectural'. You can't go wrong with the shirts, coats and suits.
40 Thomas Street, T 831 7125

Renegade Marmalade

After three years of success in a Northern Quarter cellar, womenswear boutique Renegade Marmalade moved to the seat of the Manchester fashion establishment in King Street. The store champions independent designers, and some of the stock is Manchester-born, such as JABiO, Pretty Disturbia and Boda, as well as its own line. It occupies two floors of a Georgian residence, decorated with new and antique furniture and commissioned artwork, with partners Lissom & Muster (T 0845 894 9080) on another. Originally an equestrian outfitter, L&M now has a broader focus, using British textiles such as Cumbrian wool, Macclesfield silk and Northamptonshire leather. There are plans to open a café on the ground floor. *33 King Street, T 834 5733, www.renegade-marmalade.co.uk*

Hervia Bazaar

Oscar Pinto's first Manchester store, in the Royal Exchange, was a trailblazer for the city, stocking Alexander McQueen and Vivienne Westwood. It was destroyed in the IRA bombing, but Pinto went on to open seven Westwood outlets in the UK. With this Spring Gardens project he has returned to the multi-brand blueprint. Pinto's inspiration for the interior was art deco cinema, and the store is decorated with a Murano glass chandelier, a curved Lumaglass wall, mirrored ceiling panels and brass cabinets from the Dorchester in London. The clever shelving units are a collaboration with local firm Ferrious. There's a mix of mens- and womenswear by both new and established designers, including Viktor & Rolf and Gareth Pugh. *40 Spring Gardens, T 835 2777, www.herviabazaar.com*

SPORTS AND SPAS
WORK OUT, CHILL OUT OR JUST WATCH

Manchester's football teams are two of its top draws. Old Trafford (Sir Matt Busby Way, T 868 8000) has been a source of pilgrimage for United fans for decades, and Etihad Stadium (Sportcity, T 444 1894) is the home of upstarts City, said to be the richest club in the world following the takeover by Sheikh Mansour of Abu Dhabi. If you can't get hold of a match ticket, both clubs offer tours.

The legacy of the 2002 Commonwealth Games is a wealth of world-class sporting facilities, in a city that already had its fair share, thanks to venues such as the Velodrome (see p090). The National Squash Centre (Gate 13, Rowsley Street, Sportcity, T 220 3800) and the Aquatics Centre (see p094) have remained popular both with spectators and participants. In summer, swimmers can train in the old dock at the Salford Watersports Centre (15 The Quays, T 877 7252, register at www.salford.gov.uk). The city's industrial past has left behind plenty of atmospheric canal paths for joggers to pound, whereas cyclists could try the former railway route, the Fallowfield Loop, or head out to the Cheshire Plain.

Manchester lacks an independent spa presence, though those in the Radisson (see p027) and The Lowry (see p017) hotels are top notch. Cheshire, however, has two destination pampering palaces in Rookery Hall (Main Road, Worleston, T 0845 072 7533) and the Doubletree by Hilton (Warrington Road, Chester, T 01244 408 840). *For full addresses, see Resources.*

Manchester Climbing Centre

The Greater Manchester area is relatively flat, so city climbers were delighted with the opening of this indoor facility in 2004. Architect JS Crowther's late 19th-century Italianate church has been turned into one of Europe's largest climbing centres, with a 20m main wall, 75 top-roped and lead lines, bouldering areas and a traversing room. It's a pleasingly incongruous setting for a clamber, among huge, prow-shaped stained-glass windows. One-hour sessions are available, as are masterclasses with Dave Barrans, one of the UK's top climbers. There's also a shop and a mezzanine café. *St Benedict's Church, Bennett Street, T 230 7006, www.manchesterclimbingcentre.com*

National Cycling Centre
In 2011, the 10,200 sq m National Indoor
BMX Centre, designed by EWA, was
added to FaulknerBrowns' velodrome,
where RV Webb's 250m Siberian pine
track has produced numerous world
records since opening in 1994. Arrange
a one-hour taster session on a Dolan
bike (£11) or watch Team GB train.
*Stuart Street, T 223 2244,
www.nationalcyclingcentre.com*

Razor 34

This male-grooming salon in an 1855 mill has a laidback, members' club atmosphere thanks to Staffordshire interior designers Killer5. Added to the original structural features are bold Britpop-style graphics, antique cases, chesterfield sofas, Andrew Martin's library-print wallpaper and original album covers hung on the walls.
34 Charlotte Street, T 238 8997

Aquatics Centre

This Olympic-size pool complex was built for the 2002 Commonwealth Games. Architects FaulknerBrowns did well to fit the multi-faceted venue into a compact brownfield site, placing one of the pools in the basement due to the small footprint, and its popularity as a public baths has justified the £32m spent. In fact, with a facility of this size and quality – deck-level water in the two 50m pools and one diving pool – being able to do your lengths here is like having a kickabout at Old Trafford. The centre is the home of British Water Polo, and hosts a hi-tech gym with cardio and strength-training sections, two saunas, a steam room and a hot tub. It's located in the Rainy City's university district, infamous for its traffic-related puddle-drenching incidents, so be careful you're not sick of water before you arrive.

2 Booth Street East, T 275 9450, www.manchestersportandleisure.org

ESCAPES

WHERE TO GO IF YOU WANT TO LEAVE TOWN

Urbanites shouldn't miss Manchester's great rival, Liverpool, 50km up the road. Highlights include the Metropolitan Cathedral (see p100) and numerous contemporary art venues, such as the Open Eye photography gallery (19 Mann Island, T 0151 709 9460) and the Bluecoat (School Lane, T 0151 702 5324). From Liverpool you can catch a train to Crosby to view Antony Gormley's other-worldly sculptures (see p098) or cross the Mersey to New Brighton and its art deco amusement arcade, immortalised by Martin Parr's *The Last Resort*. To get to Liverpool, those not pushed for time may fancy the six-hour ferry trip along the Ship Canal from Salford Quays (Mersey Ferries, T 0151 330 1444; only certain days, April to October) through the north-west's post-industrial backdrop.

Alternatively, head to the Pennines for some rambling. The East Lancashire section between Blackburn and Pendle is dotted with contemporary sculptures, called Panopticons, such as the *Singing Ringing Tree* by Tonkin Liu, overlooking Burnley. Its galvanised steel pipes whistle in the wind. Head north from here into Cumbria to follow Steve Coogan and Rob Brydon's foodie footsteps in *The Trip*. Delightful country restaurants L'Enclume (Cavendish Street, Grange-over-Sands, T 01539 536 362), The Samling (Ambleside Road, Windermere, T 01539 431 922) and Holbeck Ghyll (Holbeck Lane, Windermere, T 01539 432 375) are all Michelin-starred. *For full addresses, see Resources.*

Ruskin Library, Lancaster

Architects MJP were not overawed in designing this 1997 homage to John Ruskin ('When we build, let us think that we build forever'), creating an elegant structure that pays subtle tribute. Through the double-height entrance, a glass bridge unites a sequence of intimate spaces, such as the Reading Room (above), which has an ecclesiastical feel. The white concrete rendered with a marble aggregate alludes to Ruskin's love of Italian materials, and the steel plates bolted on to the curved, clean exterior are a nod to his belief that buildings should show their bones. The library houses the Whitehouse Collection of Ruskin's art and writing (Monday to Friday, 10am-4pm). It's an hour on the train to Lancaster and then a short taxi ride. *Lancaster University, Bailrigg, T 01524 593 587*

Another Place, Crosby Beach

Installed in summer 2005, the 100 iron casts of artist Antony Gormley's body were due to move to New York in late 2006, but a local campaign secured their long-term stay on Merseyside, allowing them to start the process of decay – the sea will claim them in around 150 years. The figures were joined in 2007 by the 25 turbines of the Burbo Bank offshore wind farm, and the pairing makes for a scene of peculiar beauty. With Liverpool's docks visible to the south (Crosby Beach is 20 minutes' drive from the city centre), it's apt the figures should linger here, for many would-be Irish emigrants to the US did the same in the 19th century. At the south edge of the beach, Duggan Morris Architects have plans to convert an old radar tower into the Mersey Observatory. *Burbo Bank/Waterloo Marine Lakes*

Metropolitan Cathedral, Liverpool
Implementation of Edwin Lutyens' bold
plan for this Catholic cathedral began
in 1933 but costs ballooned to £27m with
just the crypt completed. In its place
came Sir Frederick Gibberd's design,
finished in 1967, with a crown-like tower
and four approaches marked by multi-
coloured glass stelae. Empty plateaux
suggest the enormity of Lutyens' vision.
Mount Pleasant, T 0151 709 9222

The Midland, Morecambe
Architect Oliver Hill designed this art
deco hotel for Depression-era folk unable
to afford overseas travel. Its curved front
follows the sweep of the promenade (now
adorned with the Tern Project's artworks)
at the southern corner of Morecambe
Bay. It opened in 1933, and Coco Chanel
and Noël Coward were guests before
the building served as a hospital during
WWII. Urban Splash's 2008 refurbishment
produced a 44-room boutique hotel,
including six rooftop suites. Original
features were retained, such as the spiral
staircase and the seahorse-motif rugs
designed by Marion Dorn, and an Eric Gill
Odysseus stone relief was reinstalled.
The glass-walled Rotunda Bar is bathed
in light, which complements the seaside-
blue of the chairs and the huge, pale-pink
chandelier, and the spa offers an upgrade
to the traditional seaside constitutional.
Marine Road West, T 0845 850 1240

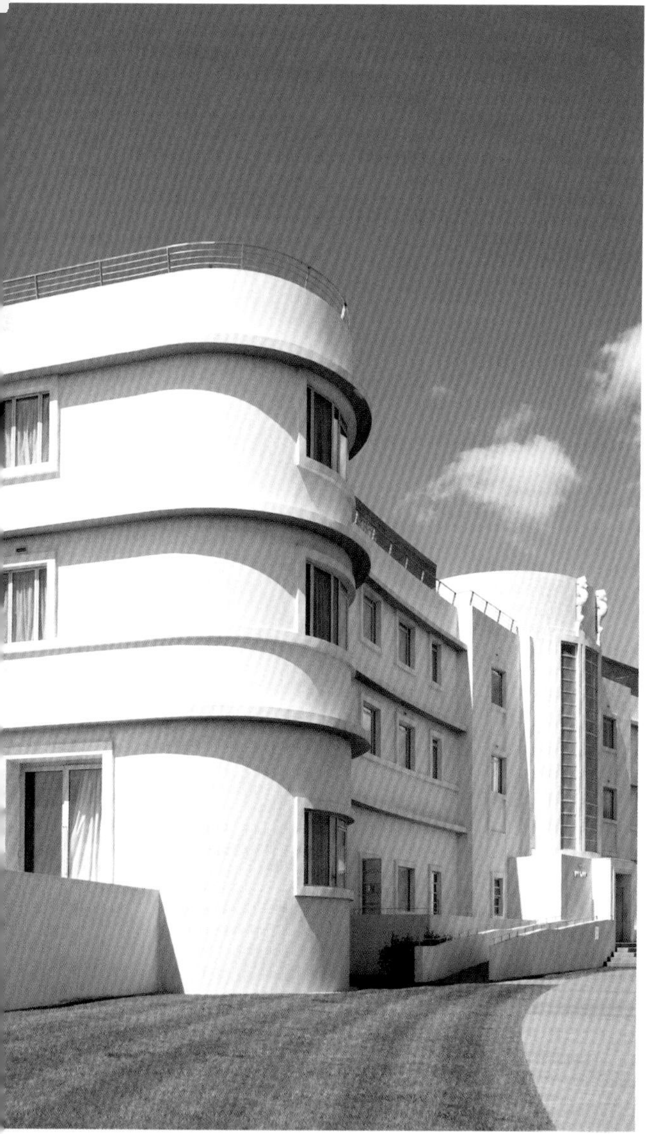

NOTES
SKETCHES AND MEMOS

RESOURCES
CITY GUIDE DIRECTORY

HOTELS

ADDRESSES AND ROOM RATES

ABode 022
  Room rates:
  double, from £90;
  Angel Suite 505, £285
  107 Piccadilly
  T 247 7744
  www.abodehotels.co.uk

Didsbury House 020
  Room rates:
  double, from £90;
  Room 40, from £175
  Didsbury Park
  Didsbury Village
  T 448 2200
  www.didsburyhouse.co.uk

Eleven Didsbury Park 016
  Room rates:
  double, from £145
  Didsbury Village
  T 448 8282
  www.elevendidsburypark.com

Great John Street 024
  Room rates:
  double, from £240;
  Eclectic Grand Suite 18, £355;
  Opus Grand Suite, £400
  Great John Street
  T 831 3211
  www.greatjohnstreet.co.uk

Hilton Deansgate 016
  Room rates:
  double, from £100
  303 Deansgate
  T 870 1600
  www.hilton.co.uk

The Light 028
  Room rates:
  double, from £85;
  penthouse, from £350
  20 Church Street
  T 839 4848
  www.thelight.co.uk

The Lowry Hotel 017
  Room rates:
  double, from £125;
  Deluxe City View room, £390;
  Riverside Suite, £970
  50 Dearmans Place
  T 827 4000
  www.thelowryhotel.com

Malmaison 016
  Room rates:
  double, from £80
  Piccadilly
  T 278 1000
  www.malmaison.com

The Midland Manchester 026
  Room rates:
  double, from £250;
  Midland Suite, £450
  Peter Street
  T 236 3333
  www.qhotels.co.uk

The Midland Morecambe 102
  Room rates:
  double, from £250
  Marine Road West
  Morecambe
  T 0845 850 1240
  www.elh.co.uk

Mint 016
  Room rates:
  double, from £115
  1 Auburn Street
  T 242 1000
  www.minthotel.com
Radisson Edwardian 027
  Room rates:
  double, from £250;
  Al Fresco Suite, £450
  Peter Street
  T 835 9929
  www.radissonedwardian.com/
  manchester
Roomzzz 028
  Room rates:
  double, from £90;
  Maxima Suite, £140;
  Penthouse Suite, £220
  36 Princess Street
  T 236 2121
  www.roomzzz.co.uk
Staying Cool 028
  Room rates:
  Fresh Apartment, from £145;
  Woody Apartment, from £175
  Hill Quays
  T 0121 285 1250
  www.stayingcool.com
Velvet 030
  Room rates:
  double, from £85;
  Velvet King 12, from £250
  2 Canal Street
  www.velvetmanchester.com

WALLPAPER* CITY GUIDES

Executive Editor
Rachael Moloney

Editor
Jeremy Case
Author
Neil McQuillian

Art Director
Loran Stosskopf

Art Editor
Eriko Shimazaki
Designer
Mayumi Hashimoto
Map Illustrator
Russell Bell

Photography Editor
Sophie Corben
Photography Assistant
Nabil Butt

Chief Sub-Editor
Nick Mee
Sub-Editors
Emily Brooks
Simon Crook
Greg Hughes

Editorial Assistant
Emma Harrison

Intern
Candace Rardon

**Wallpaper* Group
Editor-in-Chief**
Tony Chambers
Publishing Director
Gord Ray
Managing Editor
Jessica Diamond

Contributors
Lauren Atherton
Eddy Rhead

Wallpaper* ® is a
registered trademark
of IPC Media Limited

First published 2012

All prices are correct at
the time of going to press,
but are subject to change.

Printed in China

PHAIDON

Phaidon Press Limited
Regent's Wharf
All Saints Street
London N1 9PA

Phaidon Press Inc
180 Varick Street
New York, NY 10014

Phaidon® is a registered
trademark of Phaidon
Press Limited

www.phaidon.com

A CIP Catalogue record for
this book is available from
the British Library.

ISBN 978 0 7148 6295 8

PHOTOGRAPHERS

**Alan Copson/Jon Arnold/
Alamy**
Another Place, pp098-099

Peter Durant
Ruskin Library, p097

**Dennis Gilbert/
Susan Bockelmann**
Manchester city view,
inside front cover
CIS Tower, p012
Beetham Tower, p013
Hulme Arch, pp014-015
The Lowry Hotel, p017,
pp018-019
Didsbury House,
p020, p021
ABode, pp022-023
Great John Street,
pp024-025
Radisson Edwardian, p027
The Light, pp028-029
Velvet, pp030-031
North Tea Power, p033
Town Hall, p034, p035
Craft & Design
Centre, p036
Michael Caines
Restaurant, p037
Richard Goodall
Gallery, pp038-039
Chetham's Library,
p040, p041

Chill Factore, p042, p043
The Gaslamp, p044
The Deaf Institute,
pp046-047
Vertigo, p049
NoHo, pp050-051
An Outlet, p052
Aumbry, p053
Corridor, pp054-055
Albert's Shed, p056
Isinglass, p057
Vermilion and
Cinnabar, p058
Cord, p059
Obsidian, pp060-061
Pete Masters, p063
Universal Church of the
Kingdom of God, p065
Chips, pp066-067
Urbis, p068
City Airport, p070
Victoria Baths, p071
Daily Express Building,
pp072-073
John Rylands Library,
p074, p075
Barton Arcade, p076
Civil Justice Centre, p077
Hollings Faculty,
pp078-079
Oi Polloi, p081
Levenshulme Antiques
Village, pp082-083
James Darby, p084, p085
Renegade Marmalade,
p086

Hervia Bazaar, p087
Manchester Climbing
Centre, p089
National Cycling
Centre, pp090-091
Razor 34, pp092-093
Aquatics Centre, pp094-095

Len Grant
Imperial War Museum
North, pp010-011

Hufton + Crow/View/Corbis
Liverpool Metropolitan
Cathedral, pp100-101

MANCHESTER
A COLOUR-CODED GUIDE TO THE HOT 'HOODS

OXFORD ROAD
The academic centre of Manchester is a draw for its cultural venues and lively scene

PICCADILLY
Rail passengers now get a proper welcome thanks to the ongoing Piccadilly Basin project

THE QUAYS
Salford's successful docklands regeneration boasts a plethora of landmark buildings

GAY VILLAGE
Canal Street and its environs have morphed into a kicking nightlife hub for all persuasions

CASTLEFIELD
The canalside warehouses were reborn in the 1990s but Granada's exit is a new blow

CITY CENTRE
Among the shops and malls you'll find a timeline of the city's architectural development

SPINNINGFIELDS
The Civil Justice Centre spearheads a contemporary quarter that's now coming into its own

NORTHERN QUARTER
A hip enclave of independent boutiques, craft markets, art galleries, cafés and bars

For a full description of each neighbourhood, see the Introduction.
Featured venues are colour-coded, according to the district in which they are located.